April Fool's Day

Written by Cheryl Palin
Illustrated by Ángeles Peinador

On Monday morning Simon wakes up.
His brother, Matthew, is ready for school.

What time is it, Matthew?

It's half past eight.

Simon is in a hurry. He can't find his socks. He can't find his T-shirt.

Half past eight! Oh no! I'm late for school. Where are my clothes?

Matthew and Dad are in the kitchen. Breakfast is ready. Simon is dressed now. But he is wearing different socks.

Come on, Matthew! Quick! It's time for school.

Ha! Ha! You're not late for school, Simon! Look!

Simon looks at the clock. It isn't time for school. It's only eight o'clock.

Today is 1st April. It's April Fool's Day.

Dad, Simon and Matthew have breakfast. They drink hot milk and they eat toast and boiled eggs. Then they hear a knock at the door.

Matthew opens the door. But nobody is there.

But it isn't a ghost. It's Becky. Becky lives in the house next door.

Simon, Matthew and Becky walk to school. Suddenly they see something on the ground. It's a coin.

But Becky can't pick the coin up.
It's stuck to the ground with glue.

It's another April Fool trick!

All the children like April Fool's Day.

Do you want a peanut, Sophie?

Yes please, Nicholas! I love peanuts.

April Fool!

The pupils are in the classroom.
It's time for English.

Then it's time for Maths.

13

It's half past eleven. Mr Black the Maths teacher has got some paper and pencils.

OK, everyone. Listen, please! It's time for the Maths test.

The pupils are not very happy.
They don't like Maths tests.

Then Mr Black laughs. The pupils are surprised.

And now it's 12 o'clock. The children can't play any more April Fool tricks until next year.

Activities

1 Read and write T (true) or F (false).

1 Simon is late for school.   F

2 Becky knocks on the door.   _____

3 Becky can pick up the coin.   _____

4 Sophie likes peanuts.   _____

5 It's snowing on April Fool's Day.   _____

6 Mr Black is the English teacher.   _____

7 The pupils have a Maths test.   _____

8 The April Fool tricks finish at 12 o'clock.   _____

2 Look and write.

1 __toast_____

2 _____ _____

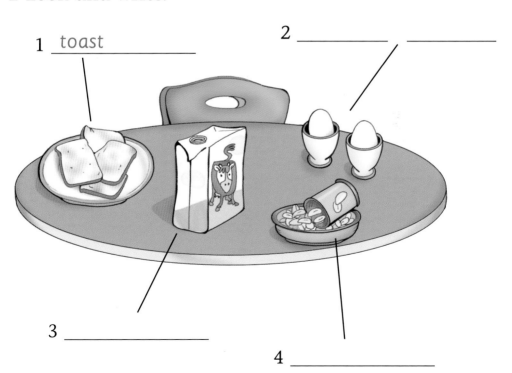

3 _____

4 _____

3 Read and match.

It's half past eight.

Do you want a peanut?

Look! It's money! I'm rich!

It's snowing!

It's time for the Maths test.

I love peanuts.

4 Look and write.

1 It's eight o'clock.   2 _____   3 _____

4 _____   5 _____   6 _____

5 Look at the story again. Find and write.

1 A green and white school bag is on _page 12_____.

2 An orange basketball is on _____.

3 A blue and yellow notebook is on _____.

4 A black and white cat is on _____.

5 A pink sun hat is on _____.

6 A black and white trainer is on _____.

6 Write and find the secret word.

maths	peanuts	door	eight	glue
friends	coin	snow	clock	

What's the secret word?

_____

7 Read and colour.

Simon is wearing an orange T-shirt and blue jeans.
He's wearing red and white trainers and black socks.

8 Look and write.

Sophie is wearing _____

_____

She's _____

_____

9 Choose and write five sentences about picture A and five sentences about picture B.

_____   _____

_____   _____

_____   _____

_____   _____

_____   _____

The door is open.

Becky can't pick up the coin.

A frog isn't in the lunchbox.

It's three o'clock.

A spider is in Simon's school bag.

Becky can pick up the coin.

A spider is on Simon's head.

It's four o'clock.

A frog is in the lunchbox.

The door is closed.

Picture Dictionary

wake up

school

half past eight

eight o'clock

late

socks

T-shirt

clothes

house

kitchen

breakfast

April

toast

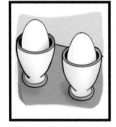

boiled eggs

milk

peanuts

door ghost coin money

glue classroom window pencil

paper Maths It's snowing. It's sunny.

laugh pick up knock surprised

Macmillan Education
Between Towns Road, Oxford OX4 3PP
A division of Macmillan Publishers Limited
Companies and representatives throughout the world

ISBN 978 1 4050 6889 5
ISBN 978 1 4050 7411 7 (International Edition)

Illustrated by Ángeles Peinador

Printed and bound in China

2011 2010 2009
10 9 8 7   Spain
10 9 8   International